# Accounting for
# Earnings per Share

Steven M. Bragg

**AccountingTools®**

ISBN 978-1-64221-305-8

For more information about AccountingTools® products, visit our Web site at www.accountingtools.com.

# Table of Contents

# About the Author

**Steven Bragg, CPA,** has been the chief financial officer or controller of four companies, as well as a consulting manager at Ernst & Young. He received a master's degree in finance from Bentley College, an MBA from Babson College, and a Bachelor's degree in Economics from the University of Maine. He has been a two-time president of the Colorado Mountain Club, and is an avid alpine skier, mountain biker, and certified master diver. Mr. Bragg resides in Centennial, Colorado. He has written more than 300 books and courses, including *New Controller Guidebook*, *GAAP Guidebook*, and *Payroll Management*.

Steven maintains the accountingtools.com web site, which contains continuing professional education courses, the Accounting Best Practices podcast, and thousands of articles on accounting subjects.

---

### Buy Additional AccountingTools Courses

AccountingTools offers more than 1,500 hours of CPE courses, with concentrations in accounting, auditing, finance, taxation, and ethics. Related courses that you might like include:

- Investor Relations Guidebook
- Public Company Accounting and Finance

Go to accountingtools.com/cpe to view these additional courses.

**AccountingTools®**

---

# Accounting for Earnings per Share

## Introduction

If a company is publicly-held, it is required to report earnings per share information. A publicly-held entity is an organization whose debt or equity securities are traded on an exchange or the over-the-counter market, or which is required to file reports with the Securities and Exchange Commission (SEC). The investment community and financial press closely follow earnings per share information, considering it to be a key view of corporate profitability.

Two types of earnings per share information are to be reported within the financial statements, which are basic and diluted earnings per share. In this manual, we describe how to calculate both basic and diluted earnings per share, as well as how to present this information within the financial statements.

A privately-held organization does not have to report earnings per share information. The earnings per share requirements also do not apply if a company has taken itself private; that is, its securities no longer trade on an exchange or in the over-the-counter market. These requirements also do not apply to the financial statements of wholly-owned subsidiaries.

## Basic Earnings per Share

Basic earnings per share is the amount of a company's profit or loss for a reporting period that is available to the shares of its common stock that are outstanding during a reporting period. It is intended to measure the performance of the reporting organization over a specific reporting period. If a business only has common stock in its capital structure, it presents only its basic earnings per share for income from continuing operations and net income. The formula for basic earnings per share is:

$$\frac{\text{Profit or loss attributable to common equity holders of the parent business}}{\text{Weighted average number of common shares outstanding during the period}}$$

In addition, subdivide this calculation for presentation purposes into:

- The profit or loss from continuing operations attributable to the parent company
- The total profit or loss attributable to the parent company

When compiling earnings per share information for the consolidated financial statements of a parent company and its subsidiaries, one may find that certain subsidiaries are less than wholly-owned, which means that there is a noncontrolling interest in these subsidiaries. If so, the income from continuing operations and net income information used to compile the basic earnings per share information should exclude all income from continuing operations and net income that are attributable to the noncontrolling interest.

When calculating basic earnings per share, incorporate into the numerator an adjustment for dividends. Deduct from the profit or loss the after-tax amount of any dividends declared on non-cumulative preferred stock (even if not yet paid), as well as the after-tax amount of any preferred stock dividends, even if the dividends are not declared; this does not include any dividends paid or declared during the current period that relate to previous periods.

Also, incorporate the following adjustments into the denominator of the basic earnings per share calculation:

- *Contingent stock*. If there is contingently issuable stock, treat it as though it were outstanding as of the date when there are no circumstances under which the shares would *not* be issued. This means it should not be possible for basic earnings per share to be restated due to changing circumstances. For example, if an earnout provision is included in a business combination, the contingent issuance of stock to the owners of the acquiree will not be included in basic earnings per share until it is certain that they will receive more shares.
- *Shares issuable for minimal consideration*. If shares can be issued for little consideration (or none at all), consider them to be outstanding common shares that are added to the denominator of the earnings per share calculation. These shares should be added as of the date when any associated conditions of issuance have been satisfied.
- *Weighted-average shares*. Use the weighted-average number of shares during the period in the denominator. This is done by adjusting the number of shares outstanding at the beginning of the reporting period for common shares repurchased or issued in the period. This adjustment is based on the proportion of the days in the reporting period that the shares are outstanding.

There may be cases in which a business issues a stock dividend, which is when a dividend is paid with stock, rather than cash or other assets. When such a dividend is issued for preferred stock, deduct this dividend from net income when computing the amount of income available to the holders of common stock. Or, if there has been a loss, add it back to the net loss.

---

**EXAMPLE**

Lowry Locomotion earns a profit of $1,000,000 net of taxes in Year 1. In addition, Lowry owes $200,000 in dividends to the holders of its cumulative preferred stock. Lowry calculates the numerator of its basic earnings per share as follows:

$$\$1,000,000 \text{ Profit} - \$200,000 \text{ Dividends} = \underline{\$800,000}$$

Lowry had 4,000,000 common shares outstanding at the beginning of Year 1. In addition, it sold 200,000 shares on April 1 and 400,000 shares on October 1. It also issued 500,000 shares on July 1 to the owners of a newly-acquired subsidiary. Finally, it bought back 60,000 shares on December 1. Lowry calculates the weighted-average number of common shares outstanding as follows:

| Date | Shares | Weighting (Months) | Weighted Average |
|---|---|---|---|
| January 1 | 4,000,000 | 12/12 | 4,000,000 |
| April 1 | 200,000 | 9/12 | 150,000 |
| July 1 | 500,000 | 6/12 | 250,000 |
| October 1 | 400,000 | 3/12 | 100,000 |
| December 1 | -60,000 | 1/12 | -5,000 |
| | | | 4,495,000 |

Lowry's basic earnings per share calculation is:

$800,000 adjusted profits ÷ 4,495,000 weighted-average shares = $0.18 per share

## Diluted Earnings per Share

Diluted earnings per share is the profit for a reporting period per share of common stock outstanding during that period; it includes the number of shares that would have been outstanding during the period if the company had issued common shares for all potential dilutive securities outstanding during the period. Several types of dilutive securities are:

- *Convertible bonds.* Can be traded in for common stock, which eliminates the related amount of interest expense but increases the number of common shares outstanding.
- *Convertible preferred stock.* Can be traded in for common stock, which eliminates the related preferred stock dividends, but increases the number of common shares outstanding.
- *Stock options.* Gives the holder (an employee) the right to buy a certain number of common shares from the company in exchange for the payment of an exercise price. This increases the cash reserves of the company, but also increases the number of common shares outstanding.
- *Warrants.* Gives the holder (a third party) the right to buy a certain number of common shares from the company in exchange for the payment of an exercise price. This increases the cash reserves of the company, but also increases the number of common shares outstanding.

As was the case for basic earnings per share, diluted earnings per share is intended to measure the performance of the reporting organization over a specific reporting period; however, the objective is more expansive, since it also incorporates all dilutive potential common shares that were outstanding during the reporting period.

If a company has more types of stock than common stock in its capital structure, it must present both basic earnings per share and diluted earnings per share information; this presentation must be for both income from continuing operations and net income. This information is reported on the company's income statement.

To calculate diluted earnings per share, include the effects of all dilutive potential common shares. This means that the shares outstanding are increased by the weighted average number of additional common shares that would have been outstanding if the company had converted all dilutive potential common stock to common stock. This dilution may affect the profit or loss in the numerator of the dilutive earnings per share calculation. The formula is:

$$\frac{\text{(Profit or loss attributable to common equity holders of parent company} + \text{After-tax interest on convertible debt} + \text{Convertible preferred dividends} \pm \text{Other changes)}}{\text{(Weighted average number of common shares outstanding during the period} + \text{All dilutive potential common stock)}}$$

It may be necessary to make several adjustments to the *numerator* of this calculation. They are:

- *Interest expense.* If there is convertible debt outstanding in the period, it is presumed to be converted into common stock. If so, add back to the numerator any interest charged that would have been associated with the debt in the reporting period[1]. This add-back of interest expense will result in a higher income level, which may in turn trigger additional changes in the numerator, such as increased profit-sharing or royalty expenses that are calculated based on the income level. Further, these changes may require a change in the amount of income tax recognized in the period, which alters the net income figure used in the numerator. These changes are made as of the beginning of the reporting period or at the time of issuance of the debt, if later.

---

**EXAMPLE**

Lowry Locomotion earns a net profit of $2 million, and it has 5 million common shares outstanding. In addition, there is a $1 million convertible loan that has an eight percent interest rate. The loan may potentially convert into 500,000 of Lowry's common shares. Lowry's incremental tax rate is 35 percent.

---

[1] However, for convertible debt for which the principal is required to be paid in cash, the interest charges shall not be added back to the numerator.

Lowry's basic earnings per share is $2,000,000 ÷ 5,000,000 shares, or $0.40/share. The following calculation shows the compilation of Lowry's diluted earnings per share:

| | |
|---|---:|
| Net profit | $2,000,000 |
| + Interest saved on $1,000,000 loan at 8% | 80,000 |
| - Reduced tax savings on foregone interest expense | -28,000 |
| = Adjusted net earnings | $2,052,000 |
| | |
| Common shares outstanding | 5,000,000 |
| + Potential converted shares | 500,000 |
| = Adjusted shares outstanding | 5,500,000 |
| | |
| Diluted earnings per share ($2,052,000 ÷ 5,500,000 shares) | **$0.37/share** |

- *Dividends*. If there is convertible preferred stock outstanding in the period, these shares are presumed to be converted into common stock. If so, it is also necessary to add back to the numerator the preferred dividends that are no longer being paid out. These changes are made as of the beginning of the reporting period or at the time of issuance of the preferred stock, if later.
- *Other changes*. There may be other changes in the reported income or loss that would result from the conversion of potential common shares into common stock. For example, a profit sharing expense might change if a conversion were to occur.

The preceding changes to the numerator should not be made if the effect would be antidilutive. This situation arises when the dividend declared in the current period for common shares is greater than the basic earnings per share figure. The effect is also antidilutive when the amount of dividends accumulated through the current period is greater than the basic earnings per share figure. The latter situation only arises when an organization has neglected to pay declared dividends for a period of time.

It may be necessary to make additional adjustments to the *denominator* of the diluted earnings per share calculation. They are:

- *Anti-dilutive shares*. If there are any contingent stock issuances that would have an anti-dilutive impact on earnings per share, do not include them in the calculation. This situation arises when a business experiences a loss, because including the dilutive shares in the calculation would reduce the loss per share. It can also occur when there are anti-dilutive contracts, such as a purchased put option that requires an issuer to buy back its shares. An anti-dilutive contract is always excluded from the diluted earnings per share calculation.

- *Dilutive shares*. If there is potentially dilutive common stock, add all of it to the denominator of the diluted earnings per share calculation. Unless there is more specific information available, assume that these shares are issued at the beginning of the reporting period.
- *Dilutive securities termination*. If a conversion option lapses during the reporting period for dilutive convertible securities, or if the related debt is extinguished during the reporting period, the effect of these securities should still be included in the denominator of the diluted earnings per share calculation for the period during which they were outstanding.

In addition to these adjustments to the denominator, also apply all of the adjustments to the denominator already noted for basic earnings per share.

---

**Tip:** The rules related to diluted earnings per share appear complex, but they are founded upon one principle – that you are trying to establish the absolute worst-case scenario to arrive at the smallest possible amount of earnings per share. If you are faced with an unusual situation involving the calculation of diluted earnings per share and are not sure what to do, that rule will likely apply.

---

In addition to the issues just noted, here are a number of additional situations that could impact the calculation of diluted earnings per share:

- *Most advantageous exercise price*. When calculating the number of potential shares that could be issued, do so using the most advantageous conversion rate from the perspective of the person or entity holding the security to be converted.
- *Settlement assumption*. If there is an open contract that could be settled in common stock or cash, assume that it will be settled in common stock, but only if the effect is dilutive. The presumption of settlement in stock can be overcome if there is a reasonable basis for expecting that settlement will be partially or entirely in cash.
- *Option exercise*. The treasury stock method is used to determine the effects of a presumed option or warrant exercise on diluted earnings per share. See the following section for more information.
- *Put options*. If there are purchased put options, only include them in the diluted earnings per share calculation if the exercise price is higher than the average market price during the reporting period.
- *Written put options*. If there is a written put option that requires a business to repurchase its own stock, include it in the computation of diluted earnings per share, but only if the effect is dilutive. If the exercise price of such a put option is above the average market price of the company's stock during the reporting period, this is considered to be "in the money," and the dilutive effect is to be calculated using the reverse treasury method, which is described in the following section.

- *Call options*. If there are purchased call options, only include them in the diluted earnings per share calculation if the exercise price is lower than the market price.

---

**Tip:** There is only a dilutive effect on the diluted earnings per share calculation when the average market price is greater than the exercise prices of any options or warrants.

---

- *Contingent shares in general*. Treat common stock that is contingently issuable as though it was outstanding as of the beginning of the reporting period, but only if the conditions have been met that would require the company to issue the shares. If the conditions were not met by the end of the period, then include in the calculation, as of the beginning of the period, any shares that would be issuable if the end of the reporting period were the end of the contingency period, and the result would be dilutive.
- *Contingent shares dependency*. If there is a contingent share issuance that is dependent upon the future market price of the company's common stock, include the shares in the diluted earnings per share calculation, based on the market price at the end of the reporting period; however, only include the issuance if the effect is dilutive. If the shares have a contingency feature, do not include them in the calculation until the contingency has been met.
- *Issuances based on future earnings and stock price*. There may be contingent stock issuances that are based on future earnings *and* the future price of a company's stock. If so, the number of shares to include in diluted earnings per share should be based on the earnings to date and the current market price as of the end of each reporting period. If both earnings and share price targets must be reached in order to trigger a stock issuance and both targets are not met, then do not include any related contingently issuable shares in the diluted earnings per share calculation.
- *Issuances based on other conditions*. If stock is to be issued based on some other condition than earnings or market price, the number of contingent shares to include in diluted earnings per share is based on the assumption that the current performance situation will remain unchanged through the end of the contingency period. Examples of these other conditions are issuing a certain number of new products or opening a certain number of new retail stores.

---

**EXAMPLE**

Lethal Sushi has 1,000,000 shares of common stock outstanding at the beginning of the year. Its fiscal year is the same as the calendar year. Lethal Sushi acquires Hunter's Delight, which specializes in the preparation of game meats. Under the terms of the business combination, the former owners of Hunter's Delight will receive an additional 10,000 shares of Lethal common stock for every new restaurant that Hunter's Delight opens in the current year. This is a contingent stock agreement. A new restaurant is opened on February 1 and another on March 1. In the first quarter, the combined entity earned $500,000. The following table illustrates the resulting calculation of basic and diluted earnings per share.

| | First Quarter EPS Calculations |
|---|---|
| **Basic earnings per share computation:** | |
| Numerator | $500,000 |
| Denominator: | |
| Common shares outstanding | 1,000,000 |
| Restaurant opening contingency (1) | 10,000 |
| Total shares | 1,010,000 |
| Basic earnings per share | <u>$0.50</u> |
| | |
| **Diluted earnings per share computation:** | |
| Numerator | $500,000 |
| Denominator: | |
| Common shares outstanding | 1,000,000 |
| Restaurant opening contingency (2) | 20,000 |
| Total shares | 1,020,000 |
| Diluted earnings per share | <u>$0.49</u> |

(1) 10,000 shares are issued on February 1 and another 10,000 shares on March 1. The calculation for contingent shares in the basic earnings per share calculation is: (10,000 shares × 2/3) + (10,000 shares × 1/3)

(2) The calculation of diluted earnings per share for contingent shares includes the restaurant-triggered shares as of the *beginning* of the quarter.

---

- *Compensation in shares*. If employees are awarded shares that have not vested or stock options as forms of compensation, then treat these grants as options when calculating diluted earnings per share (but only if the related service condition has been rendered). Consider these grants to be outstanding on the grant date, rather than any later vesting date. The resulting presumed increase in shares should be included in the diluted earnings per share calculation, but only if there is a dilutive effect. This dilutive effect is calculated using the treasury stock method, which is described in the next section. When using the treasury stock method, assume that the proceeds from these compensation arrangements include all of the following:

  - The exercise price paid by the employee
  - The amount of compensation cost associated with services to be provided in the future, and not yet recognized
  - Any excess tax benefits that would be added to additional paid-in capital if the options were to be exercised; this is the deduction caused

by any compensation in excess of the compensation expense recognized in the income statement

Always calculate the number of potential dilutive common shares independently for each reporting period presented in the financial statements.

## Treasury Stock and Reverse Treasury Stock Methods

The preceding section addressed the calculation of diluted earnings per share. The dilutive effects of certain types of securities are dealt with using the treasury stock method or the reverse treasury stock method. These calculations are noted in the following sub-sections.

### Treasury Stock Method

When an organization has outstanding call options or warrants, their dilutive effects are calculated using the treasury stock method. This method employs the following sequence of assumptions and calculations:

1. Assume that options and warrants are exercised at the beginning of the reporting period. If they were actually exercised later in the reporting period, use the actual date of exercise.
2. The proceeds garnered by the presumed option or warrant exercise are assumed to be used to purchase common stock at the average market price during the reporting period.
3. The difference between the number of shares assumed to have been issued and the number of shares assumed to have been purchased is then added to the denominator of the computation of diluted earnings per share.

In Step 2 of the process, the average market price during a quarterly reporting period is based on the average market prices during all three months of the reporting period. A simple average of weekly or monthly closing market prices is usually sufficient for this calculation. When prices fluctuate considerably, it might instead be necessary to use an average of the high and low prices for the reporting period.

When the year-to-date average pricing is determined, it is based on the year-to-date weighted average number of incremental shares included in each quarterly earnings per share computation.

The treasury stock method will only have a dilutive effect when the average market price of the common stock in the period is greater than the exercise price of the options or warrants.

The following example illustrates the concept.

**EXAMPLE**

Lowry Locomotion earns a net profit of $200,000, and it has 5,000,000 common shares outstanding that sell on the open market for an average of $12 per share. In addition, there are 300,000 options outstanding that can be converted to Lowry's common stock at $10 each.

Lowry's basic earnings per share is $200,000 ÷ 5,000,000 common shares, or $0.0400 per share.

Lowry's controller wants to calculate the amount of diluted earnings per share. To do so, he follows these steps:

1. *Calculate the number of shares that would have been issued at the market price.* Thus, he multiplies the 300,000 options by the average exercise price of $10 to arrive at a total of $3,000,000 paid to exercise the options by their holders.
2. *Divide the amount paid to exercise the options by the market price to determine the number of shares that could be purchased.* Thus, he divides the $3,000,000 paid to exercise the options by the $12 average market price to arrive at 250,000 shares that could have been purchased with the proceeds from the options.
3. *Subtract the number of shares that could have been purchased from the number of options exercised.* Thus, he subtracts the 250,000 shares potentially purchased from the 300,000 options to arrive at a difference of 50,000 shares.
4. *Add the incremental number of shares to the shares already outstanding.* Thus, he adds the 50,000 incremental shares to the existing 5,000,000 to arrive at 5,050,000 diluted shares.

Based on this information, the controller arrives at diluted earnings per share of $0.0396, for which the calculation is:

$200,000 Net profit ÷ 5,050,000 Common shares

This method may also be used when a business has issued the following instruments:

- Nonvested stock granted to employees
- Stock purchase contracts
- Partially paid stock subscriptions

**Reverse Treasury Stock Method**

A business may be party to a contract that requires it to buy back its own stock from a shareholder. This type of arrangement is called a put option. If the effect of a put option is dilutive (which occurs when the exercise price is higher than the average market price in a reporting period), it must be included in the diluted earnings per share calculation. The calculation of the effect of a put option is measured using the reverse treasury stock method, which involves the following steps:

1. Assume that enough shares were issued by the company at the beginning of the period at the average market price to raise sufficient funds to satisfy the put option contract.
2. Assume that these proceeds are used to buy back the required number of shares.
3. Include in the denominator of the diluted earnings per share calculation the difference between the numbers of shares issued and purchased in steps 1 and 2.

---

**EXAMPLE**

A third party exercises a written put option that requires Armadillo Industries to repurchase 1,000 shares from the third party at an exercise price of $30. The current market price is $20. Armadillo uses the following steps to compute the impact of the written put option on its diluted earnings per share calculation:

1. Armadillo assumes that it has issued 1,500 shares at $20.
2. The company assumes that the "issuance" of 1,500 shares is used to meet the repurchase obligation of $30,000.
3. The difference between the 1,500 shares issued and the 1,000 shares repurchased is added to the denominator of Armadillo's diluted earnings per share calculation.

---

## Two-Class Method

There may be situations in which an entity issues securities with special features that are designed to attract investors, such as preferred stock that participates in the dividends issued to common stockholders. There may also be several classes of common stock that have different dividend rates. For example, the holders of certain preferred shares might receive a multiple of the dividends paid to common shareholders. There could also be a cap on the amount of these extra dividends. These special securities are called *participating securities*.

The two-class method is used to allocate earnings to participating securities, without requiring that basic or diluted earnings per share be presented for them if the securities are of a type other than common stock. One can report earnings per share for these participating securities that are not common stock, but it is not required.

The calculation methodology for the two-class method covers the following steps:

1. Reduce the amount of income from continuing operations by the dividends declared in the reporting period for each class of stock, and by the contractually-mandated dividends that must be paid for the current period.
2. Allocate the remaining earnings to common stock and the participating securities to the extent that the securities agreement allows for such a distribution.
3. Divide the amount allocated to each security by the number of outstanding shares of the security, to arrive at the earnings per share for the security.
4. Present basic and diluted earnings per share for each class of common stock.

It is possible that losses should also be allocated to a participating security if there is a contractual obligation for the security to share in the losses. This is considered to be the case when the holder is obligated to fund the losses of the issuer, or when the mandatory redemption amount of the security is reduced by the amount of the loss.

All participating securities are to be included in the calculation of basic earnings per share under this two-class method.

---

**EXAMPLE**

Sawtooth Corporation has the following capital structure:

- 100,000 shares of common stock
- 20,000 shares of Series A preferred stock

The Series A stock is entitled to a $2 annual dividend before any dividends are paid on the common stock. In addition, the Series A stock is to participate in any additional dividends on a 10:90 per-share ratio with common stock, once a $0.10 dividend has been paid on the common stock.

Sawtooth reports $200,000 of net income. In the period, the board of directors authorizes a total of $60,000 in dividends. The breakdown of payments is that Series A stockholders are paid $41,000 and the common stockholders are paid $19,000; these amounts are derived from the following table:

| Share Type | Number of Shares | | Base-Level Dividend | | Base-Level Aggregate Dividend | | Additional Dividend (90:10) | | Total Dividend | Per Share |
|---|---|---|---|---|---|---|---|---|---|---|
| Common | 100,000 | × | $0.10/share | = | $10,000 | + | $9,000 | = | $19,000 | $0.19 |
| Series A | 20,000 | × | $2.00/share | = | 40,000 | + | 1,000 | = | 41,000 | $2.05 |
| Totals | 120,000 | | | | $50,000 | | $10,000 | | $60,000 | |

Sawtooth calculates its undistributed earnings as follows:

| | | |
|---|---|---|
| Net income | | $200,000 |
| Less dividends paid: | | |
| Common | $19,000 | |
| Series A | 41,000 | |
| Undistributed earnings | | $140,000 |

Based on the 10:90 ratio at which the Series A stock participates in any additional undistributed earnings, the basic earnings per share amounts for the two types of stock are as follows:

|  | Common Stock | Series A Preferred Stock |
| --- | --- | --- |
| Distributed earnings | $0.19 | $2.05 |
| Undistributed earnings (1)(2) | 1.26 | 0.70 |
| Totals | $1.45 | $2.75 |

(1) Undistributed earnings for common stock is calculated as: ($140,000 × 90%) ÷ 100,000 shares

(2) Undistributed earnings for Series A stock is calculated as: ($140,000 × 10%) ÷ 20,000 shares

## Master Limited Partnerships

A master limited partnership is a limited partnership that is publicly traded on an exchange. It may issue several classes of securities to investors, where the securities participate in the earnings of the partnership. The calculation of the participation is included in the partnership agreement. The ownership interests of such a partnership typically include the following elements:

- Common units that are held by limited partners, and which are publicly traded; and
- An interest held by the general partner; and
- Incentive distribution rights.

Incentive distribution rights may be structured as a nonvoting limited partner interest, and are held by the general partner. Depending on the terms of these rights, they may be an integral part of the general partner's interest, or they may be transferrable to a third party.

In a master limited partnership, the governing partnership agreement typically requires the general partner to distribute all available cash following the end of each reporting period to the partners. The calculation of this distribution is made using a distribution waterfall, which specifies the amounts to be paid out at different threshold levels. Above a designated threshold, some funding is also allocated to the incentive distribution rights, which represents a bonus to the general partner or whoever is now holding the rights.

When the partnership generates a net income or loss, it is allocated to the capital accounts of the partners based on the income and loss sharing percentages stated in the partnership agreement. These allocations are made after taking into account any income allocations made to the incentive distribution rights.

The following discussion of earnings per share for a master limited partnership only applies when both of the following conditions are present:

- The partnership must issue incentive distributions when certain thresholds have been surpassed; and
- These incentive distributions are accounted for as equity distributions by the partnership, rather than compensation costs.

Incentive distribution rights are considered to be participating securities, as described earlier for the two-class method. Accordingly, the two-class method described in the preceding section is to be used to calculate earnings per unit. The method should also be used for the general partner and limited partner interests, since they are considered separate classes of equity.

## Presentation and Disclosure of Earnings per Share

The following sub-sections describe how earnings per share information is to be presented in the financial statements, as well as the types of additional disclosures that must be presented.

### Presentation Issues

The basic and diluted earnings per share information is normally listed at the bottom of the income statement, and is included for every period in the income statement. Both earnings per share figures should be displayed with equal prominence. Also, if diluted earnings per share information is reported in *any* of the periods included in a company's income statement, it must then be reported for *all* of them. The following sample illustrates the concept.

### Sample Presentation of Earnings per Share

| Earnings per Share | 20x3 | 20x2 | 20x1 |
|---|---|---|---|
| **From continuing operations** | | | |
| Basic earnings per share | $1.05 | $0.95 | $0.85 |
| Diluted earnings per share | 1.00 | 0.90 | 0.80 |
| | | | |
| **From discontinued operations** | | | |
| Basic earnings per share | $0.20 | $0.17 | $0.14 |
| Diluted earnings per share | 0.15 | 0.08 | 0.07 |
| | | | |
| **From total operations** | | | |
| Basic earnings per share | $1.25 | $1.12 | $0.99 |
| Diluted earnings per share | 1.15 | 0.98 | 0.87 |

**Tip:** There is no specific requirement in Generally Accepted Accounting Principles (GAAP) to use the terms "basic earnings per share" or "diluted earnings per share" in the income statement. For example, "earnings per common share" could be used instead. Whatever terms are employed, we suggest using them consistently over time, to prevent confusion.

Note that, if the company reports a discontinued operation, it must present the basic and diluted earnings per share amounts for this item. The information can be included either as part of the income statement or in the accompanying notes. The preceding sample presentation includes a disclosure for earnings per share from discontinued operations.

**Tip:** If the amounts of basic and diluted earnings per share are the same, it is allowable to have a dual presentation of the information in a single line item on the income statement.

If there is a stock split or reverse stock split, this increases or decreases (respectively) the number of shares outstanding. If so, the computations of basic and diluted earnings per share are to be retroactively adjusted for all periods being reported, so that all periods reflect the change in the total number of shares outstanding.

### EXAMPLE

In the past year, Hammer Industries reported basic and diluted earnings per share of $1.44 and $0.88, respectively. At the beginning of the next year, Hammer issues a 4 for 1 stock split. This means that the denominator of its basic and diluted earnings per share calculations has just quadrupled. When Hammer next issues financial statements, the prior year earnings per share information will be reduced to one fourth of their former amounts, which will be $0.36 for its basic earnings per share and $0.22 for its diluted earnings per share.

### Disclosure Issues

In addition to the earnings per share presentation requirements just noted, a company is also required to report the following information:

- *Reconciliation.* State the differences between the numerators and denominators of the basic and diluted earnings per share calculations for income from continuing operations.
- *Preferred dividends effect.* State the effect of preferred dividends on the computation of income available to common stockholders for basic earnings per share.
- *Potential effects.* Describe the terms and conditions of any securities not included in the computation of diluted earnings per share due to their antidilutive effects, but which could potentially dilute basic earnings per share in the future.

**SAMPLE DISCLOSURE**

For the years ended December 31, 20X4, 20X3 and 20X2, there were approximately 9 million, 12 million and 29 million, respectively, of outstanding stock awards that were not included in the computation of diluted earnings per share because their effect was antidilutive.

- *Subsequent events*. Describe any transactions occurring after the latest reporting period but before the issuance of financial statements that would have a material impact on the number of common or potential common shares if they had occurred prior to the end of the reporting period. Examples of these situations are:
  - o Issuance of common stock
  - o Issuance of options or warrants
  - o Resolution of a contingency in a contingent stock agreement
  - o Conversion of potential common stock into common stock

If an entity must restate the results of its operations for a prior period, then the related earnings per share information must also be restated. The effect of the restatement must be disclosed, expressed in per-share terms.

A business may choose to report additional per-share amounts that are not required by GAAP. If so, they should be disclosed only in the notes to the financial statements, not on the income statement. Also, such an additional presentation should state whether the per share information is before tax or after tax.

**Note:** Reporting an amount of cash flow per share anywhere in the financial statements or the accompanying notes is not allowed.

Do not retroactively adjust previously reported information for diluted earnings per share, if there have been subsequent conversions, or subsequent changes in the market price of the common stock. In effect, prior diluted earnings per share information is considered to be frozen from a reporting perspective.

## Non-GAAP Disclosures

Some publicly-held companies want to present the best possible version of their results to the investment community, and do so by selectively disclosing only the better portions of their actual financial results. This can result in the presentation of earnings per share information that is higher than the normal results. Such information is considered to be a non-GAAP financial measure by the SEC, which defines such information as follows:

> A non-GAAP financial measure is a numerical measure of a registrant's historical or future financial performance, financial position or cash flows that:
> (i)   Excludes amounts, or is subject to adjustments that have the effect of excluding amounts, that are included in the most directly comparable measure calculated and presented in accordance with GAAP in the statement of income, balance sheet or statement of cash flows (or equivalent statements of the issuer); or
> (ii)  Includes amounts, or is subject to adjustments that have the effect of including amounts, that are excluded from the most directly comparable measure so calculated and presented.
>
> A non-GAAP financial measure does not include operating and other financial measures and ratios or statistical measures calculated using exclusively one or both of;
> (i)   Financial measures calculated in accordance with GAAP; and
> (ii)  Operating measures or other measures that are not non-GAAP financial measures.

The result of issuing non-GAAP financial measures can be misleading, when compared to the actual results reported under GAAP. To mitigate the effects of this misleading information, the SEC's Regulation G requires certain additional disclosures. The following text is taken from the Regulation:

> a.   Whenever a registrant … publicly discloses material information that includes a non-GAAP financial measure, the registrant must accompany that non-GAAP financial measure with:
> 1.   A presentation of the most directly comparable financial measure calculated and presented in accordance with GAAP; and
> 2.   A reconciliation … of the differences between the non-GAAP financial measure disclosed or released with the most comparable financial measure or measures calculated and presented in accordance with GAAP.
> b.   A registrant, or a person acting on its behalf, shall not make public a non-GAAP financial measure that, taken together with the information accompanying that measure and any other accompanying discussion of that measure, contains an untrue statement of a material fact or omits to state a material fact necessary in order to make the presentation of the non-GAAP financial measure, in light of the circumstances under which it is presented, not misleading.

In summary, the SEC requires that any non-GAAP financial measures (such as a modified earnings per share figure) disclosed by a company must be accompanied by a ιeconciliation to a financial measurement that has been calculated using GAAP, and it should not be misleading. This means that non-GAAP financial measures can still be released; it is up to the reader of the presented information to examine the accompanying reconciliation and decide if the non-GAAP information is relevant to his or her investing needs.

## Summary

It will have been evident from the discussions of earnings per share that the computation of diluted earnings per share can be quite complex if a business has a correspondingly complex equity structure. In such a situation, it is quite likely that diluted earnings per share will be incorrectly calculated. To improve the accuracy of the calculation, create an electronic spreadsheet that incorporates all of the necessary factors impacting diluted earnings per share. Further, save the calculation for each reporting period on a separate page of the spreadsheet; by doing so, there will be an excellent record of how these calculations were managed in the past.

# Glossary

**A**

*Antidilution.* When an increase in earnings per share or decrease in loss per share occurs.

**B**

*Basic earnings per share.* The amount of earnings in a reporting period that is available to the common shares outstanding in that period.

**C**

*Call option.* A contract that allows its holder to buy a fixed number of shares at a fixed price within a designated date range.

*Common stock.* Shares that are subordinate to all other classes of stock of the issuer.

*Contingent issuance.* An issuance of shares that may occur if certain conditions are satisfied.

*Contingently issuable shares.* Shares that are issuable if certain conditions are met, and requiring a minimal cash payment.

*Conversion rate.* The ratio of common shares to be issued to each unit of a convertible security.

*Convertible security.* A security that can be converted into another security at a defined conversion rate.

**D**

*Diluted earnings per share.* The amount of earnings in a reporting period that is available to the common shares outstanding and all shares that would have been outstanding if all dilutive common shares had been issued.

**E**

*Earnings per share.* The amount of earnings or losses in a reporting period that can be apportioned to each share of common stock.

*Exercise price.* The amount that the holder of an option or warrant must pay for a share of common stock when the option or warrant is exercised.

**O**

*Option.* A right that gives its holder the option to purchase shares of common stock at a certain price and within a specific date range.

**P**

*Participating security.* A security that can receive undistributed earnings along with common stock, of which the most common example is sharing in dividends.

*.ential common stock.* A security or agreement that allows its holder to obtain common stock during or after a reporting period.

*Preferred stock.* An equity security that has preferential rights in comparison to common stock.

*Put option.* A contract that allows its holder to sell a certain number of shares to the originator of the contract at a fixed price within a designated date range.

## W

*Warrant.* A security that gives its holder the right to buy a certain number of shares at a fixed price within a designated date range.

# Index

www.ingramcontent.com/pod-product-compliance
Lightning Source LLC
Chambersburg PA
CBHW051431200326
41520CB00023B/7432